I0797510

Dinks *and* Drinks

Dinks and

A Pickleball Cocktail Book

CHRONICLE BOOKS
SAN FRANCISCO

Drinks

Recipes by
CAMILLE WILSON

Photography by
ERICA ALLEN

Library of Congress Cataloging-in-Publication Data available.

ISBN 978-1-7972-3595-0

Manufactured in China.

Design by Vanessa Dina.
Recipes by Camille Wilson.

Recipes on pages 34–35, 44–45, 54–55, 70–71, 80–81, and 92–93 by Chronicle Books.
Photography by Erica Allen.
Food and beverage styling by Skylar Edberg.
Prop styling by Amy Taylor.
Assistant styling by Kendra Aronson.
Typeset in Mabry Pro.

10 9 8 7 6 5 4 3 2 1

Chronicle books and gifts are available at special quantity discounts to corporations, professional associations, literacy programs, and other organizations. For details and discount information, please contact our premiums department at corporatesales@chroniclebooks.com or at 1-800-759-0190.

Chronicle Books LLC
680 Second Street
San Francisco, California 94107
www.chroniclebooks.com

Recipes

Introduction

What could be more perfect than a gorgeous, sunny day filled with rounds of pickleball with friends and rounds of well-crafted cocktails to toast your game? Whether you're courtside or just seeking pickleball vibes at your next soiree, this collection of cocktails serves what you need. All 42 of these recipes are inspired by pickleball phrases and terminology:

Whip up a refreshing cucumber-infused Backspin Spritz between games.

Share a glass of Centerline Punch while waiting for a free court.

Bring a bunch of Spicy Golden Pickles to your next après-pickleball gathering.

So grab your paddle and your cocktail shaker and mix up some delicious drinks. See you in the kitchen and on the court!

Bar Tools

Here's a list of key cocktail equipment and items you should pack in your gear bag for optimal cocktail making.

Barspoon: Used for stirring drinks. It's long enough to reach the bottom of a shaker or deep serving glass with ease.

Citrus Press: The best cocktails are made with freshly squeezed citrus juice (never bottled!). A citrus press makes juicing a breeze.

Glassware: Different sorts of glassware speak to different styles of cocktails. A coupe glass, flute, highball glass, julep cup, low-ball or rocks glass, and wineglass are always good to have on hand.

Jigger: You'll need this to accurately measure ingredients. It might be tempting to eyeball measurements, but to make the most balanced cocktail, opt for accuracy.

Muddler: A handy tool to crush cocktail ingredients in a shaker and better infuse their flavors into your drink.

Peeler: Used for creating delicate citrus garnishes. Y-shaped and straight peelers are both great options, so pick whichever you're most comfortable with.

Shaker: Look for a Boston or cobbler shaker. The Boston is the simpler of the two (two cups put together). The cobbler is an all-in-one shaker, with a cup, strainer, and lid. So if you want to invest more in your cocktail game, go for the cobbler.

Strainer: There are many types of strainers out there, but the Hawthorne is standard. It's ideal for straining out ice and other mix-ins like muddled herbs and fruit.

Pickleball Bar Cart

Although all of these won't fit into your paddle bag, keep a mix of these bar ingredients on hand for easy pickleball cocktail making.

Alcohol

Brandy: Distilled from wine or other fermented fruit, brandy can have a pleasant, sweet, oaky flavor.

Gin: Made from juniper berries, this clear liquor is fragrant and surprisingly versatile.

Rum: Created by fermenting and then distilling sugarcane juice, rum typically comes in two varieties: White rum is usually either unaged or aged briefly in stainless-steel tanks, while dark rum is typically aged in charred oak barrels, which create the amber color and richer flavor.

Tequila: Made from the blue agave plant, tequila, much like wine, can vary in flavor notes depending on where the agave is cultivated, but it tends to have a smooth, lightly sweet, and earthy quality.

Vodka: One of the most popular alcohol varieties, vodka has a neutral taste that makes it incredibly versatile and can be used with a range of mixers, flavors, and ingredients.

Whiskey: Warm in color and flavor, whiskey has lots of variations based on the location it's made in. One popular variety is bourbon, which tends to have notes of vanilla and caramel.

Liqueurs + Other Alcohols

Aperitifs: You've probably had or at least heard of Aperol, the most famous of the category. Used in combination with sparkling water or wine, aperitif-based drinks offer a delightfully complex flavor profile without the need to add many other mixers and ingredients.

Beer: Keep a stash of beers in your paddle bag to quickly assemble a radler or other beer-based drink (like the Pickle-ada on page 70), or simply crack an icy cold one to enjoy between games on a hot afternoon.

Bitters: Use these super concentrated extracts with a light hand to add a punch of flavor.

Liqueurs: Liqueurs (not to be confused with liquors) are alcohols with added sugars that come in an array of flavors. The recipes in this book use a selection of liqueurs, including banana liqueur, elderflower liqueur, and orange liqueur.

Wines: Wine, specifically white and sparkling, offer a lovely, aged flavor to drinks without adding too much alcohol or overpowering the whole drink.

Mixers + Nonalcoholic Liquids

Fresh fruit juices: It's always best to use freshly squeezed juice over prepackaged, especially lemon, lime, and any other citrus juices. But for rarer or hard-to-find juices like mango, watermelon, pineapple, cherry, and yuzu, it's OK to buy store-bought (sometimes simplicity is best).

Fizzy drinks: Sometimes all you need to make a drink sing is a fizzy base. Sparkling water is of course the most neutral of all the fizzy mixers, but explore others like spicy ginger beer or herby tonic water.

Sweeteners

Simple syrup: The gold standard of sweeteners for cocktail making. You can buy premade versions but it's ideal to make your own (see page 21). It has a nice, clean sweetness, which makes it perfect for infusing with other flavors like cherry, honeydew, and more (see pages 21–25 for more syrup recipes).

Agave syrup: Made from the same plant used for tequila production, agave has a reliable smooth consistency, and some believe that it's slightly healthier than standard sugar syrups. Much like simple syrup, it can easily be infused with other flavors, using similar techniques as those used in the simple syrup infusions found in this book.

Grenadine: When you want your drink to pop with a vibrant red color and candy-like sweetness, reach for grenadine.

Garnishes

Fruit: Used as a pretty garnish, plopped into a drink, or muddled with other cocktail ingredients, fruit (and sometimes veggies!) adds a puckery, fresh element that visually completes a drink. For fruits and veggies like limes, lemons, and cucumbers, try serving them a bunch of different ways like wedges, peels, and wheels. For smaller fruits like blueberries, cherries, and ginger pieces, artfully place them on a cocktail pick to rest on the rim of the glass. Or go for the maximalist look and mix a bunch of small fruits straight into your drink. For fleshier fruits like peaches, pineapples, or watermelon, a wedge lightly pushed onto the rim of a glass so it balances on top works well. Bonus: Grill select fruits briefly to impart more complex flavor notes.

Herbs: A sprig or sprinkle of fresh leaves adds a verdant vibe to any cocktail. Pro tip: Grow yourself a cocktail herb garden with herbs like basil, mint, and more so you always have fresh garnishes on hand.

Rims: Cocktail rims require a bit of extra effort, but it's worth it to have a fun and playful topper on a well-crafted drink. See page 27 for detailed instructions on how to properly rim your cocktail glass. The world of rimming elements is diverse: Start with some granulated sugar, salt, edible flowers, or toasted coconut.

Extras: Sometimes a drink needs an extra little something to give it that oomph. Select drinks in this book employ back-pocket ingredients to make you look like a pickleball mixologist: egg whites or aquafaba to make drinks frothy and light, a dusting of spices like nutmeg for a spicy finish, and butterfly pea tea for a natural blue-to-purple hue.

Syrups

Take your pickleball cocktail game to the next level with these easy and elevated syrups that you'll use to make the recipes in this book.

Simple Syrup

MAKES 1½ CUPS [360 ML]

1 cup [200 g] sugar
1 cup [240 ml] water

In a small saucepan over medium heat, combine the sugar and water. Stir until the sugar is dissolved. Remove from the heat and let cool.

Store in a resealable container in the refrigerator for up to 4 weeks.

Blueberry Syrup

MAKES 2 CUPS [475 ML]

1 cup [200 g] sugar
1 cup [240 ml] water
1 cup [140 g] blueberries

In a small saucepan over medium heat, combine the sugar and water. Stir until the sugar is dissolved. Add the blueberries and bring to a low boil. Decrease the heat and let simmer for 15 minutes. Remove from the heat and let cool before straining into a container.

Store in a resealable container in the refrigerator for up to 2 weeks.

Brown Sugar Pineapple Syrup

MAKES 1½ CUPS [360 ML]

1 cup [240 ml] pineapple juice
1 cup [200 g] brown sugar

In a small saucepan over medium heat, combine the juice and sugar. Stir until the sugar is dissolved. Remove from the heat and let cool.

Store in a resealable container in the refrigerator for up to 2 weeks.

Cherry Syrup

MAKES 2 CUPS [475 ML]

1 cup [200 g] sugar
1 cup [240 ml] water
1 cup [70 g] pitted and halved cherries

In a small saucepan over medium heat, combine the sugar and water. Stir until the sugar is dissolved. Add the cherries and bring to a low boil. Decrease the heat and let simmer for 10 minutes. Remove from the heat and let cool before straining into a container.

Store in a resealable container in the refrigerator for up to 2 weeks.

Cucumber Syrup

MAKES 2 CUPS [475 ML]

1 cup [200 g] sugar
1 cup [240 ml] water
1 cup [140 g] peeled and chopped cucumbers

In a small saucepan over medium heat, combine the sugar and water. Stir until the sugar is dissolved. Add the cucumber and bring to a low boil. Decrease the heat and let simmer for 10 minutes. Remove from the heat and let cool before straining into a container.

Store in a resealable container in the refrigerator for up to 2 weeks.

Honey Syrup

MAKES 2 CUPS [475 ML]

1 cup [340 g] honey
1 cup [240 ml] warm water

In a small bowl, whisk together the honey and warm water until the honey is dissolved.

Store in a resealable container in the refrigerator for up to 4 weeks.

Honeydew Mint Syrup

MAKES 1½ CUPS [360 ML]

1 cup [140 g] honeydew melon chunks
1 cup [200 g] sugar
1 cup [12 g] mint leaves

Blend the honeydew melon chunks in a blender or food processor and strain to remove any solids. In a small saucepan over medium heat, combine the melon juice and sugar. Stir until the sugar is dissolved. Add the mint leaves and bring to a low boil. Turn off the heat and let steep for 5 to 10 minutes.

Store in a resealable container in the refrigerator for up to 2 weeks.

Passion Fruit Syrup

MAKES 2 CUPS [475 ML]

1 cup [200 g] sugar
1 cup [240 ml] water
1 cup [240 ml] fresh or frozen passion fruit purée

In a small saucepan over medium heat, combine the sugar and water. Stir until the sugar is dissolved. Stir in the passion fruit purée and cook for 5 minutes. Remove from the heat and let cool before straining into a container.

Store in a resealable container in the refrigerator for up to 2 weeks.

Peach Syrup

MAKES 2 CUPS [475 ML]

1 cup [200 g] sugar
1 cup [240 ml] water
1 cup [140 g] sliced peaches

In a small saucepan over medium heat, combine the sugar and water. Stir until the sugar is dissolved. Add the peach slices and bring to a low boil. Decrease the heat and let simmer for 5 minutes. Remove from the heat and let cool before straining into a container.

Store in a resealable container in the refrigerator for up to 2 weeks.

Pear Ginger Syrup

MAKES 2 CUPS [475 ML]

1 cup [200 g] sugar
1 cup [240 ml] water
1 cup [140 g] peeled and chopped pears
½ cup [70 g] sliced fresh ginger

In a small saucepan over medium heat, combine the sugar and water. Stir until the sugar is dissolved. Add the pears and ginger and bring to a low boil. Decrease the heat and let simmer for 10 minutes. Remove from the heat and let cool before straining into a container.

Store in a resealable container in the refrigerator for up to 2 weeks.

Watermelon Syrup

MAKES 1½ CUPS [360 ML]

1 cup [240 ml] watermelon juice
1 cup [200 g] sugar

In a small saucepan over medium heat, combine the watermelon juice and sugar. Stir until the sugar is dissolved. Remove from the heat and let cool before straining into a container.

Store in a resealable container in the refrigerator for up to 2 weeks.

How to Rim a Glass

Want to take your perfectly crafted cocktail to the next level? Coating the rim of your drink's glass can be the visual cherry on top and adds an extra dimension of flavor with each sip. You can rim your glass with the standard salt and sugar, but the sky's the limit on what else you can use: Think dried flowers, spices, toasted coconut, or sprinkles.

To rim your glass, wet the rim of your drinking glass with water or fruit juice. On a small plate, add your rimming ingredient (sugar, salt, etc.). Dip the prepared glass upside down into the mixture, rotating to coat fully.

Backspin Spritz

3 oz [90 ml] chilled sparkling wine

½ oz [15 ml] elderflower liqueur

1 oz [30 ml] Cucumber Syrup (page 22)

1 oz [30 ml] sparkling water

Edible flowers, for garnish

Cucumber ribbon, for garnish

In a wineglass with ice, add the sparkling wine, elderflower liqueur, syrup, and sparkling water. Stir to combine. Garnish with edible flowers and cucumber and serve.

Backspin: When a player applies spin to the ball by hitting it in a high-to-low swing, sometimes called a slice, causing the ball to spin in the opposite direction of its trajectory.

Sideline Sip

1½ oz [45 ml] blanco tequila

½ oz [15 ml] orange liqueur

1 oz [30 ml] Passion Fruit Syrup (page 24)

½ oz [15 ml] fresh lime juice

Lime wheel, for garnish

To a shaker, add the tequila, orange liqueur, syrup, lime juice, and ice. Shake until chilled and strain into a lowball glass with ice. Garnish with a lime wheel and serve.

MAKES 1 DRINK

Sideline: The line perpendicular to the net marking the edge of the court.

Midcourt Margarita

Salt or sugar, for the rim

Lime zest, for the rim

2 oz [60 ml] blanco tequila

¾ oz [22.5 ml] orange liqueur

1½ oz [45 ml] guava nectar

¾ oz [22.5 ml] fresh lime juice

¾ oz [22.5 ml] coconut water

Lime wheel, for garnish

On a small plate, stir together the salt or sugar and lime zest. Wet the rim of a lowball or margarita glass with water and dip it upside down into the mixture, rotating to coat fully. Set aside.

To a shaker, add the tequila, orange liqueur, guava nectar, lime juice, coconut water, and ice. Shake until chilled and strain into the prepared glass with ice. Garnish with a lime wheel and serve.

MAKES 1 DRINK

Midcourt: The court area between the non-volley zone and the baseline.

Rosé Rally

One 750 ml bottle rosé

3 oz [90 ml] fresh lemon juice

3 oz [90 ml] Honey Syrup (page 23)

1 cup [140 g] hulled and chopped strawberries, plus more for garnish

Pour the rosé into ice cube trays and freeze overnight. To a blender, add the frozen rosé cubes, lemon juice, syrup, strawberries, and a handful of ice. Blend until smooth, then divide between six coupes or wineglasses. Garnish each glass with a strawberry and serve.

MAKES 6 DRINKS

Rally: A continuous back-and-forth play between teams during a game.

Pickletini

2 oz [60 ml] vodka

1 oz [30 ml] pickle brine

½ oz [15 ml] dry vermouth

Cornichon, for garnish

To a shaker, add the vodka, pickle brine, vermouth, and ice. Shake until very chilled and strain into a martini glass. Garnish with the cornichon.

MAKES 1 DRINK

Dillball Sparkler

2 oz [60 ml] chilled sparkling wine

3 oz [90 ml] cooled, freshly brewed butterfly pea tea

1 oz [30 ml] Simple Syrup (page 21)

¾ oz [22.5 ml] yuzu juice

Mint sprig, for garnish

In a highball glass with ice, add the sparkling wine, tea, syrup, and yuzu juice. Stir to combine, garnish with the mint, and serve.

MAKES 1 DRINK

Dillball: A live/in-play ball.

Pickle Spritz in a Can

One 12 oz [360 ml] can of sparkling water

1 oz [30 ml] vodka

1 oz [30 ml] mango juice

½ oz [15 ml] fresh lime juice

½ oz [15 ml] Simple Syrup (page 21)

Mint sprig, for garnish

Pour out about 8 oz [240 ml] of sparkling water from the can so 4 oz [120 ml] remain. Set aside. Remove the top of the can using a can cutter top remover. To the opened can, add the vodka, mango juice, lime juice, syrup, and ice. Stir to combine. Garnish with a mint sprig and serve.

MAKES 1 DRINK

Fault So Fresh

4 or 5 strawberries, hulled, plus 1 whole strawberry, for garnish

¾ oz [22.5 ml] Simple Syrup (page 21)

5 or 6 mint leaves

1 oz [30 ml] coconut rum

½ oz [15 ml] fresh lime juice

2 oz [60 ml] sparkling water

Lime wheel, for garnish

In a shaker, muddle the hulled strawberries, syrup, and mint leaves. Add the rum, lime juice, and ice. Shake until chilled and strain into a lowball glass with ice. Add the sparkling water. Garnish with a strawberry and lime wheel and serve.

MAKES 1 DRINK

Fault: A violation of the rules that stops play.

Peach Honey Lob

½ peach, sliced, plus more for garnish

¾ oz [22.5 ml] Honey Syrup (page 23)

1½ oz [45 ml] vodka

¼ oz [7.5 ml] fresh lemon juice

1 oz [30 ml] sparkling water

In a shaker, muddle the peach slices and syrup. Add the vodka, lemon juice, and ice. Shake until chilled and strain into a lowball glass with ice. Add the sparkling water. Garnish with a peach slice or two and serve.

MAKES 1 DRINK

Lob: A very high shot with a rounded trajectory that lands deep on the opponent's side of the court.

Dink 'n' Stormy

2 oz [60 ml] rum
½ oz [15 ml] fresh lime juice
4 oz [120 ml] ginger beer
Lime wheel, for garnish
Candied ginger, for garnish

In a highball glass with ice, add the rum and fresh lime juice. Add the ginger beer and stir to combine. Garnish with a lime wheel and candied ginger and serve.

MAKES 1 DRINK

Dink: A soft shot that lands in the opponent's non-volley zone (a.k.a. the kitchen).

Mimosa Float

1 to 2 scoops orange sherbet

6 oz [180 ml] chilled Champagne

2 oz [60 ml] fruit juice, such as orange, passion fruit, or pineapple juice

Orange slice, for garnish

Scoop the orange sherbet into a highball glass. Pour the Champagne and juice over the top. Garnish with an orange slice and serve with a wide straw and spoon.

MAKES 1 DRINK

Spritz & Serve

- 2 oz [60 ml] chilled sparkling wine
- 1 oz [30 ml] vodka
- 1½ oz [45 ml] sparkling water
- 1 oz [30 ml] Cherry Syrup (page 22)
- Cherries, for garnish

In a wineglass with ice, add the sparkling wine, vodka, sparkling water, and syrup. Stir to combine. Garnish with fresh cherries and serve.

MAKES 1 DRINK

Serve: The initial strike of the ball with the paddle to start the rally.

Dink Daiquiri

1 oz [30 ml] white rum

1 oz [30 ml] dark rum

1 oz [30 ml] Brown Sugar Pineapple Syrup (page 22)

¾ oz [22.5 ml] fresh lime juice

Grilled pineapple wedge, for garnish

To a shaker, add the white rum, dark rum, syrup, lime juice, and ice. Shake until chilled and strain into a coupe glass to serve up or a wineglass with ice. Garnish with a grilled pineapple wedge and serve.

MAKES 1 DRINK

Dink: A soft shot that lands in the opponent's non-volley zone (a.k.a. the kitchen).

The Green Paddle

1½ oz [45 ml] gin

1 oz [30 ml] Honeydew Mint Syrup (page 23)

1 oz [30 ml] fresh lime juice

Mint sprig, for garnish

Honeydew melon balls, for garnish

To a shaker, add the gin, syrup, lime juice, and ice. Shake until chilled and strain into a coupe glass. Garnish with a mint sprig and honeydew melon balls and serve.

MAKES 1 DRINK

Paddle: The racket used to hit the pickleball.

Basil on the Baseline

4 basil leaves, plus more for garnish

2 oz [60 ml] watermelon juice

2 oz [60 ml] chilled sparkling wine

1 oz [30 ml] sparkling water

Watermelon slice, for garnish

In a wineglass, muddle the basil leaves and watermelon juice. Add the sparkling wine, sparkling water, and ice. Stir to combine, garnish with basil leaves and a watermelon slice, and serve.

MAKES 1 DRINK

Baseline: The line parallel to the net marking the back edge of the court.

Forehand Float

2 oz [60 ml] vanilla vodka

6 oz [180 ml] root beer

1 or 2 scoops vanilla ice cream

Whipped cream, for garnish

Maraschino cherry, for garnish

In a highball glass, add the vodka and root beer and stir to combine. Add the vanilla ice cream. Garnish with a swirl of whipped cream and a cherry on top.

MAKES 1 DRINK

Forehand: A shot on a player's dominant side using the front face of the paddle.

Beer & Cheer Squad

One 12 oz [360 ml] can frozen limeade concentrate, such as Minute Maid

Four 12 oz [360 ml] bottles Corona (or other Mexican beer)

6 oz [180 ml] tequila

3 oz [90 ml] Grand Marnier or triple sec

Lime wedges, for garnish

In a large pitcher, add the frozen limeade concentrate, beer, tequila, and Grand Marnier. Stir to combine. Divide between four or five highball glasses, garnish each with a lime wedge, and serve.

MAKES A PITCHER

4–5
DRINKS

Peach Pickle

2 oz [60 ml] dark rum

¼ oz [7.5 ml] Peach Syrup (page 24)

3 dashes aromatic bitters

Orange peel, for garnish

Peach slice, for garnish

In a mixing glass, combine the rum, syrup, and bitters. Stir to combine and strain into a lowball glass with ice. Garnish with an orange peel and peach slice and serve.

MAKES 1 DRINK

Centerline Punch

16 oz [480 ml] dark rum

8 oz [240 ml] fresh lime juice

8 oz [240 ml] sparkling water

6 oz [180 ml] mango juice

6 oz [180 ml] Simple Syrup (page 21)

2 oz [60 ml] pineapple juice

2 oz [60 ml] grenadine

1½ tsp aromatic bitters

Pineapple fronds, for garnish

Nutmeg, for garnish

In a large pitcher, add the rum, lime juice, sparkling water, mango juice, syrup, pineapple juice, grenadine, and bitters. Stir to combine. Taste and add more sparkling water if desired. To serve, divide the mixture evenly among six to eight lowball glasses with ice. Garnish each glass with a pineapple frond and a pinch of nutmeg and serve.

MAKES A PITCHER

6–8
DRINKS

Centerline: The line between the non-volley zone and baseline.

Paddle Punch

16 oz [480 ml] blanco tequila

8 oz [240 ml] Cucumber Syrup (page 22)

8 oz [240 ml] coconut water

4 oz [120 ml] pineapple juice

4 oz [120 ml] fresh lime juice

4 oz [120 ml] water

Pineapple wedges, for garnish

Cucumber wheels, for garnish

In a large pitcher, add the tequila, syrup, coconut water, pineapple juice, lime juice, and water. Stir to combine. Taste and add more water if desired. To serve, divide the mixture evenly among six to eight lowball glasses with ice. Garnish each glass with a pineapple wedge and cucumber wheel and serve.

MAKES A PITCHER

6–8 DRINKS

Reset Refresher

One 750 ml bottle dry white wine

4 oz [120 ml] brandy

2 oz [60 ml] fresh lemon juice

2 oz [60 ml] Simple Syrup (page 21)

2 kiwis, peeled and sliced, plus more for garnish

1 lemon, sliced

1 lime, sliced

1 peach, sliced

1 cup [140 g] strawberries, hulled and sliced, plus more for garnish

In a large pitcher, add the wine, brandy, lemon juice, syrup, kiwis, lemon, lime, peach, and strawberries. Stir to combine. Refrigerate for at least 4 hours. To serve, divide the mixture evenly among six to eight lowball glasses with ice, making sure there's fruit in every glass. Garnish each glass with a kiwi slice and a strawberry and serve.

MAKES A PITCHER

6–8
DRINKS

Reset: The act of hitting the ball softly into the kitchen or non-volley zone to regain control of the point.

Court Cooler

2 oz [60 ml] blanco tequila

2 oz [60 ml] grapefruit juice

½ oz [15 ml] fresh lime juice

½ oz [15 ml] agave syrup

2 oz [60 ml] sparkling water

Grapefruit slice, for garnish

To a shaker, add the tequila, grapefruit juice, lime juice, syrup, and ice. Shake until chilled. Pour into a highball glass with ice and top with the sparkling water. Stir to combine, garnish with a grapefruit slice, and serve.

MAKES 1 DRINK

Cherry Paddy Mule

1½ oz [45 ml] vodka

3 oz [90 ml] ginger beer

1 oz [30 ml] cherry juice

¼ oz [7.5 ml] Simple Syrup (page 21)

Mint sprig, for garnish

Candied ginger, for garnish

In a copper mug or highball glass with ice, add the vodka, ginger beer, cherry juice, and syrup. Stir to combine. Garnish with a mint sprig and candied ginger and serve.

MAKES 1 DRINK

Paddy: A nickname for a paddle.

The Pickler

2 oz [60 ml] gin

¾ oz [22.5 ml] fresh lemon juice

¾ oz [22.5 ml] Pear Ginger Syrup (page 25)

1 egg white or 1 oz [30 ml] aquafaba

Pear slice, for garnish

To a shaker without ice, add the gin, lemon juice, syrup, and egg white. Shake for 15 seconds. Add ice to the shaker and shake for an additional 15 seconds. Strain into a coupe glass, garnish with a pear slice, and serve.

MAKES 1 DRINK

Pickler: A pickleball superfan.

Pickle-ada

Tajín, for the rim

Salt, for the rim

4 oz [120 ml] tomato juice

4 oz [120 ml] beer

1 Tbsp pickle brine

1 dash hot sauce

Cornichon, for garnish

On a small plate, mix together equal parts Tajín and salt for the rim. Wet the rim of a highball glass with water and dip it upside down in the Tajín-salt mixture, rotating to coat fully.

Fill the glass with ice. Add the tomato juice, beer, pickle brine, and hot sauce and stir to combine. Garnish with a cornichon and serve.

MAKES 1 DRINK

Lemon Drop Shot

Lemon slice, for garnish

Sugar

1 oz [30 ml] vodka

½ oz [15 ml] fresh lemon juice

½ oz [15 ml] Simple Syrup (page 21)

Dip the lemon slice in sugar to coat. In a shot glass, add the vodka, lemon juice, and syrup. To serve, garnish with the lemon, or shoot right away and chase with the sugared lemon slice.

MAKES 1 SHOT

Drop Shot: A soft shot that drops into the opponent's kitchen near the net.

Sideline 75

1 oz [30 ml] gin

¾ oz [22.5 ml] Watermelon Syrup (page 25)

½ oz [15 ml] fresh lemon juice

1 oz [30 ml] chilled sparkling wine

Watermelon slice, for garnish

To a shaker, add the gin, syrup, lemon juice, and ice. Shake until chilled. Strain into a Champagne flute, with ice if desired, and top with the sparkling wine. Garnish with a watermelon slice and serve.

MAKES 1 DRINK

Topspin Tipple

Turbinado sugar, for the rim

2 oz [60 ml] vodka

½ oz [15 ml] orange liqueur

1 oz [30 ml] Blueberry Syrup (page 21)

1 oz [30 ml] fresh lemon juice

Blueberries, for garnish

On a small plate, add the sugar. Wet the rim of a coupe glass with water and dip it upside down into the sugar, rotating to coat fully. Set aside.

To a shaker, add the vodka, orange liqueur, syrup, lemon juice, and ice. Shake until chilled and strain into the prepared coupe glass. Garnish with blueberries and serve.

MAKES 1 DRINK

Topspin: When a player applies spin to the ball so that it rotates in the direction of its trajectory, resulting in a faster ball and lower bounce.

Peach Basil Put Away

2 oz [60 ml] gin

¾ oz [22.5 ml] Peach Syrup (page 24)

½ oz [15 ml] fresh lemon juice

3 basil leaves, plus more for garnish

1 oz [30 ml] sparkling water

Lemon wedge, for garnish

To a shaker, add the gin, syrup, lemon juice, basil leaves, and ice. Shake until chilled. Pour into a lowball glass with ice and top with the sparkling water. Stir to combine, garnish with a lemon wedge and fresh basil leaf or two, and serve.

MAKES 1 DRINK

Put Away: A shot that is impossible to return.

Spicy Golden Pickle

Turbinado sugar, for the rim

1½ oz [45 ml] reposado tequila

½ oz [15 ml] chile poblano liqueur

½ oz [15 ml] orange liqueur

1 oz [30 ml] Brown Sugar Pineapple Syrup (page 22)

Pineapple wedge, for garnish

On a small plate, add the sugar. Wet the rim of a lowball glass with water and dip it upside down into the sugar, rotating to coat fully. Set aside.

To a shaker, add the tequila, chile poblano liqueur, orange liqueur, syrup, and ice. Shake until chilled. Pour into the prepared glass with fresh ice, garnish with a pineapple wedge, and serve.

MAKES 1 DRINK

Golden Pickle: When a team defeats their opponent using only their first server.

Aperol Approach

3 oz [90 ml] chilled prosecco

3 oz [90 ml] Aperol

1 oz [30 ml] sparkling water

2 strawberries, sliced, for garnish

Orange slice, for garnish

In a wineglass with ice, add the prosecco, Aperol, and soda water. Stir to combine. Garnish with the strawberries and an orange slice.

MAKES 1 DRINK

Approach: A strategically placed shot that allows you to approach the net.

Berry Smash

8 to 10 raspberries or blackberries, plus more for garnish

4 mint or basil leaves

2 lime wedges

2 oz [60 ml] vodka

½ oz [15 ml] Blueberry Syrup (page 21)

Sparkling water, for topping off

In a shaker, muddle together the berries, mint leaves, and lime wedges to release their juices. Add the vodka, syrup, and ice. Shake until chilled. Pour everything into a highball glass, or strain over fresh ice. Add the sparkling water and stir to combine. Garnish with additional berries to serve.

MAKES 1 DRINK

Smash: A high ball that's hit downward with force; usually very hard to return.

Volley Colada

Toasted coconut flakes, for the rim

Honey, for the rim

1½ oz [45 ml] white rum

1½ oz [45 ml] pineapple juice

1½ oz [45 ml] coconut water

½ oz [15 ml] Simple Syrup (page 21)

On a small plate, add the coconut flakes. On another small plate, add the honey. Dip a lowball glass upside down into the honey, then the coconut, rotating to coat fully. Set aside.

To a shaker, add the rum, pineapple juice, coconut water, syrup, and ice. Shake until chilled. Pour into the prepared lowball glass with fresh ice and serve.

MAKES 1 DRINK

Volley: A shot where the pickleball is hit in the air before it bounces.

Bubbly Blast Off

3 oz [90 ml] chilled sparkling wine

1½ oz [45 ml] Aperol

1 oz [30 ml] sparkling water

½ oz [15 ml] Passion Fruit Syrup (page 24)

Passion fruit seeds, for garnish

Orange peel, for garnish

In a wineglass with ice, add the sparkling wine, Aperol, sparkling water, and syrup. Stir to combine. Garnish with passion fruit seeds and an orange peel and serve.

MAKES 1 DRINK

Blast Off: When the score is 3-2-1, yell "BLAST OFF!"

Nasty Nelson Julep

1 tsp apricot jam

8 mint leaves

2 oz [60 ml] bourbon

Mint sprig, for garnish

Dried apricot, for garnish

In a shaker, muddle the jam and mint leaves. Add the bourbon and ice. Shake until chilled and pour into a julep cup or highball glass with ice. Garnish with a mint sprig and dried apricot and serve.

MAKES 1 DRINK

Nasty Nelson: When a player, while serving, hits an opponent intentionally.

Whiskey Banger

6 blueberries

5 mint leaves, plus more for garnish

½ lemon, cut into small wedges, plus a wheel for garnish

2 oz [60 ml] whiskey

¾ oz [22.5 ml] Simple Syrup (page 21)

1½ oz [45 ml] sparkling water

In a shaker, muddle the blueberries, mint leaves, and lemon wedges. Add the whiskey, syrup, and ice. Shake until chilled and strain into a lowball glass with ice. Add the sparkling water and stir to combine. Garnish with a lemon wheel and mint leaf and serve.

MAKES 1 DRINK

Banger: A player who hits hard shots.

Ace & Tonic

2 oz [60 ml] gin

4 oz [120 ml] tonic water

Frozen peach slices, for garnish

Frozen blueberries, for garnish

In a highball glass with ice, add the gin and tonic water. Stir to combine. Garnish with frozen peaches and frozen blueberries and serve.

MAKES 1 DRINK

Ace: A serve that an opponent is unable to return.

Side Out Sidecar

2 oz [60 ml] brandy

1 oz [30 ml] Cointreau

½ oz [15 ml] fresh lemon juice

Lemon peel, for garnish

To a shaker, add the brandy, Cointreau, lemon juice, and ice. Shake until chilled. Strain into a coupe glass, garnish with a lemon twist, and serve.

MAKES 1 DRINK

Side Out: When the serving team has lost the point so the other team gets to serve.

Body Shot

2 oz [60 ml] vodka

1 oz [30 ml] pineapple juice

½ oz [15 ml] Brown Sugar Pineapple Syrup (page 22)

Splash of grenadine

Pineapple wedge, for garnish

Maraschino cherry, for garnish

In a double shot glass, add the vodka, pineapple juice, and syrup and stir to combine. Add a splash of grenadine to achieve an ombré effect. Garnish with the pineapple wedge and a cherry and serve.

MAKES 1 DRINK

Body Shot: When the pickleball hits another player's body.

Cross-Court Mule

1½ oz [45 ml] dark rum

3 oz [90 ml] ginger beer

1½ oz [45 ml] watermelon juice

½ oz [15 ml] Cucumber Syrup (page 22)

Cucumber wheel, for garnish

Lime wedge, for garnish

In a copper mug with ice, add the rum, ginger beer, watermelon juice, and syrup. Stir to combine. Garnish with a cucumber wheel and lime wedge and serve.

MAKES 1 DRINK

Cross-Court: Describing something diagonally across the court, such as a cross-court shot.

Bananas for Pickleball

Toasted coconut flakes, for the rim

1½ oz [45 ml] coconut rum

½ oz [15 ml] banana liqueur

½ oz [15 ml] fresh lime juice

¼ oz [7.5 ml] Simple Syrup (page 21)

Lime wheel, for garnish

Fresh cherry, for garnish

On a small plate, add the coconut flakes. Wet the rim of a coupe glass with water and dip it upside down into the coconut, rotating to coat fully. Set aside.

To a shaker, add the rum, banana liqueur, lime juice, syrup, and ice. Shake until chilled. Strain into the prepared coupe glass, garnish with a lime wheel and cherry, and serve.

MAKES 1 DRINK

Kitchen Spritz

1 oz [30 ml] mango juice

3 basil leaves, plus more for garnish

3 oz [90 ml] chilled sparkling wine

¾ oz [22.5 ml] Simple Syrup (page 21)

¼ oz [7.5 ml] fresh lime juice

Lime wheel, for garnish

In a highball glass, muddle the mango juice and basil leaves. Add the sparkling wine, syrup, and lime juice. Stir to combine. Add ice, garnish with a basil leaf and lime wheel, and serve.

MAKES 1 DRINK

Kitchen: A nickname for the non-volley zone (the section on either side of the net that a player cannot volley from).

Make It for a Crowd

Some of the recipes in this book are already designed for sharing, but if you want to keep the party going even longer, here are a few more scaled-up versions! All of these make about a pitcher, or six to eight drinks.

Sideline Sip

12 oz [360 ml] blanco tequila
4 oz [120 ml] orange liqueur
8 oz [240 ml] Passion Fruit Syrup (page 24)
4 oz [120 ml] fresh lime juice
Lime wheels, for garnish

In a pitcher with ice, add the tequila, orange liqueur, syrup, and lime juice. Stir to combine. Pour into lowball glasses. Garnish with lime wheels and serve.

Midcourt Margarita

Salt or sugar, for the rim
Lime zest, for the rim
16 oz [480 ml] blanco tequila
6 oz [180 ml] orange liqueur
12 oz [360 ml] guava nectar
6 oz [180 ml] fresh lime juice
6 oz [180 ml] coconut water
Lime wheels, for garnish

On a small plate, stir together the salt or sugar and lime zest. Wet the rim of eight lowball glasses with water and dip them upside down into the mixture, rotating to coat fully. Set aside.

In a large pitcher with ice, add the tequila, orange liqueur, guava nectar, lime juice, and coconut water. Stir to combine. Pour into the prepared lowball glasses. Garnish with lime wheels and serve.

Peach Honey Lob

3 peaches, sliced, plus more for garnish

6 oz [180 ml] Honey Syrup (page 23)

12 oz [360 ml] vodka

2 oz [60 ml] fresh lemon juice

8 oz [240 ml] sparkling water

In a pitcher, muddle the peach slices and syrup. Add the vodka, lemon juice, sparkling water, and ice. Stir to combine. Strain into lowball glasses with ice. Garnish with peach slices and serve.

Spritz & Serve

16 oz [480 ml] chilled sparkling wine

8 oz [240 ml] vodka

12 oz [360 ml] sparkling water

8 oz [240 ml] Cherry Syrup (page 22)

Cherries, for garnish

In a pitcher, add the sparkling wine, vodka, sparkling water, and syrup. Stir to combine. Pour into wineglasses filled with ice. Garnish with fresh cherries and serve.

Basil on the Baseline

20 basil leaves, plus more for garnish

16 oz [480 ml] watermelon juice

16 oz [480 ml] chilled sparkling wine

8 oz [240 ml] sparkling water

In a pitcher, muddle the basil leaves and watermelon juice. Add the sparkling wine, sparkling water, and ice. Stir to combine. Pour into wineglasses, garnish with a basil leaf, and serve.

Court Cooler

12 oz [360 ml] blanco tequila

12 oz [360 ml] grapefruit juice

3 oz [90 ml] fresh lime juice

3 oz [90 ml] agave syrup

12 oz [360 ml] sparkling water

Grapefruit slices, for garnish

In a large pitcher, add the tequila, grapefruit juice, lime juice, syrup, and ice. Stir to combine. Pour into highball glasses and top each with the sparkling water. Stir to combine, garnish with a grapefruit slice, and serve.

Topspin Tipple

Turbinado sugar, for the rim

16 oz [480 ml] vodka

4 oz [120 ml] orange liqueur

8 oz [240 ml] Blueberry Syrup (page 21)

8 oz [240 ml] fresh lemon juice

Blueberries, for garnish

On a small plate, add the sugar. Wet the rim of coupe glasses with water and dip them upside down into the sugar, rotating to coat fully. Set aside.

In a pitcher, add the vodka, orange liqueur, syrup, lemon juice, and ice. Stir until chilled. Strain into the prepared coupe glasses. Garnish with blueberries and serve.

Volley Colada

Toasted coconut flakes, for the rim

Honey, for the rim

12 oz [360 ml] white rum

12 oz [360 ml] pineapple juice

12 oz [360 ml] coconut water

4 oz [120 ml] Simple Syrup (page 21)

On a small plate, add the coconut flakes. On another small plate, add the honey. Dip lowball glasses upside down into the honey, then the coconut, rotating to coat fully. Set aside.

In a pitcher, add the rum, pineapple juice, coconut water, and syrup. Stir to combine. Pour into the prepared lowball glasses filled with fresh ice and serve.

Glossary

Ace

A serve that an opponent is unable to return.

Approach

A strategically placed shot that allows you to approach the net.

Backspin

When a player applies spin to the ball by hitting it in a high-to-low swing, sometimes called a slice, causing the ball to spin in the opposite direction of its trajectory.

Banger

A player who hits hard shots.

Baseline

The line parallel to the net marking the back edge of the court.

Blast Off

When the score is 3-2-1, yell "BLAST OFF!"

Body Shot

When the pickleball hits another player's body.

Centerline

The line between the non-volley zone and baseline.

Cross-Court

Describing something diagonally across the court, such as a cross-court shot.

Dillball

A live/in-play ball.

Dink

A soft shot that lands in the opponent's non-volley zone (a.k.a. the kitchen).

Drop Shot
A soft shot that drops into the opponent's kitchen near the net.

Fault
A violation of the rules that stops play.

Forehand
A shot on a player's dominant side using the front face of the paddle.

Golden Pickle
When a team defeats their opponent using only their first server.

Kitchen
A nickname for the non-volley zone (the section on either side of the net that a player cannot volley from).

Lob
A very high shot with a rounded trajectory that lands deep on the opponent's side of the court.

Midcourt
The court area between the non-volley zone and the baseline.

Nasty Nelson
When a player, while serving, hits an opponent intentionally.

Paddle
The racket used to hit the pickleball.

Paddy
A nickname for a paddle.

Pickler
A pickleball superfan.

Put Away
A shot that is impossible to return.

Rally
A continuous back-and-forth play between teams during a game.

Reset
The act of hitting the ball softly into the kitchen or non-volley zone to regain control of the point.

Serve
The initial strike of the ball with the paddle to start the rally.

Sideline
The line perpendicular to the net marking the edge of the court.

Side Out
When the serving team has lost the point so the other team gets to serve.

Smash
A high ball that's hit downward with force; usually very hard to return.

Topspin
When a player applies spin to the ball so that it rotates in the direction of its trajectory, resulting in a faster ball and lower bounce.

Volley
A shot where the pickleball is hit in the air before it bounces.

Index

A

B

C

D

E

F

H

K

L

M

N

O